The Gingerbread Bakers

by Amy Moses
illustrated by Vicki Wo~~~~

Scott Foresman

Editorial Offices: Glenview, Illinois • New York, New York
Sales Offices: Reading, Massachusetts • Duluth, Georgia
Glenview, Illinois • Carrollton, Texas • Menlo Park, California

The clock rang. Ned ran into
Heather's room. "Get ready!" he yelled.

"Come back later," Heather groaned.

"But Heather," said Ned, "it's time
to get ready. We're Grandpa's
helpers today."

"I know," said Heather. "But I'm a
sleepyhead." She stretched. Then she
kicked off her bedspread and climbed
out of bed.

Heather looked out the window.

It was dark. She got dressed and
ran downstairs.

Ned, Mom, and Dad were ready to go.
They were waiting for Heather. Dad was
holding a bag of cookie cutters.

They all piled into the car. They were going to help Grandpa make gingerbread. Grandpa is a baker.

When they got to the shop, Grandpa gave everyone a big kiss on the forehead. "What would you like to bake today?" Grandpa asked.

"Gingerbread!" they all shouted.

"How about cornbread instead?"
asked Grandpa.

"No!" they all cried.

"How about shortbread?" he asked.

"No!" they all said. "We want to
make gingerbread!"

Grandpa laughed. "Go wash
your hands."

Grandpa read the cookbook.
Heather put the flour into a large bowl.
Ned added the spices. Mom put in the
honey. Dad added the eggs. Then
Grandpa turned on the mixer.

When the dough was ready,
Grandpa scraped it out of the bowl.
He cut it into smaller pieces.

They used rolling pins to make the
dough flat. Then everyone chose a
cookie cutter and started to cut out
shapes. When everyone was finished,
Grandpa put the gingerbread shapes
on baking trays.

"I'm going to be a gingerbread watcher," Heather said.

"I'm going to be a gingerbread watcher too," cried Ned. "We will tell you when it's ready."

Grandpa set the timer on the large oven.

After a while, Heather and Ned
called, "It's ready. The gingerbread
is ready."

While the gingerbread cooled, Ned
and Heather made icing.

Heather and Ned drew feathers on
the birds. They drew berries on the
trees. They drew faces on the people.

Heather and Ned were happy. They
were gingerbread bakers!

"What would you like to eat today?"
Grandpa asked.

"Gingerbread!" they all shouted.

"How about cornbread instead?"
asked Grandpa.

"No!" they all cried.

"How about shortbread?" he asked.

"No!" they all said. "We want to eat
gingerbread!"

Grandpa laughed. "Who is ready to be a gingerbread eater?"

"We are! We are!" they all cried.

Grandpa picked up a plate of gingerbread. He always made some for his helpers. "Now the gingerbread bakers are gingerbread eaters!" he said.